Other Kaplan Books for High Schoolers

High School 411

Grammar Power

Learning Power

Reading Power

Math Power

Ultimate GHSGT*

Cynthia and Drew Johnson

*Georgia High School Graduation Test

Simon & Schuster

NEW YORK · LONDON · SINGAPORE · SYDNEY · TORONTO

Kaplan Publishing
Published by Simon & Schuster
1230 Avenue of the Americas
New York, NY 10020

For bulk sales to schools, please contact: Order Department, Simon & Schuster, 100 Front Street, Riverside, NJ 08075. Phone: 1-800-223-2336. Fax: 1-800-943-9831.

Project Editor: Ruth Baygell
Contributing Editors: Marc Bernstein, Marcy Bullmaster
Cover Design: Cheung Tai
Production Manager: Michael Shevlin
Interior Page Design and Layout: Laurel Douglas
Production Editor: Maude Spekes
Managing Editor: Dave Chipps
Executive Editor: Del Franz

Manufactured in the United States of America

September 2001
10 9 8 7 6 5 4 3 2 1

ISBN: 0-7432-0500-6

All of the practice questions in this book were created by the authors to illustrate question types. They are not actual test questions. For information on the GHSGT, visit the Georgia Department of Education Web site at www.doe.k12.ga.us/sla/ret/ghsgt.asp.

TABLE OF CONTENTS

ABOUT THE AUTHORS

Cynthia and Drew Johnson

Cynthia Johnson is the author of several educational books for young people, two of which received the prestigious Parent's Choice Gold Award in 1995, and were listed in *Curriculum Administrator* magazine's "Top 100" educational products for 1996. Drew Johnson is an education writer and editor, creating workbook, textbook, and Web-based education materials for children of all ages. The Johnsons have authored *Kaplan Learning Power*, a guide for improving study skills, and Kaplan's No-Stress Guides and Parent's Guides to various statewide standardized tests.

WHY TAKING THE HIGH SCHOOL GRADUATION TEST IS LIKE DRIVING A CAR FOR THE FIRST TIME

You sit down, trying to remember all the things you know you're supposed to know. The people around you seem to be feeling the same way you are— a little nervous. An adult looks at you and points at his watch, telling you it's time to start. There's no chance of going back now: It's time to take the Georgia High School Graduation Test (GHSGT).

Navigating the GHSGT can sometimes be a confusing experience.

© 2000 Picture Quest Inc./© 2000 PhotoSpin Inc.

You're probably familiar with the Criterion-Referenced Competency Tests (CRCT) from grades seven and eight. Well, the High School Graduation Tests are similar: These multiple-choice exams probe your knowledge in five core subject areas: English language arts, writing, math, science, and social studies. And though the two tests are similar in format, the GHSGT has a much greater impact on your academic career. Georgia law makes passing this test a requirement for high school graduation. Since 1991, Georgia students have had to consider the following mathematical equations:

> Equation 1:
> You + good GHSGT scores = diploma

> Equation 2:
> You − good GHSGT scores = retake the GHSGT until you achieve a passing score on all graduation tests

You don't need to be Albert Einstein to recognize that equation 1 is more desirable than equation 2. Fortunately, though, if you fail only one subject test but pass all the others, you'll have to retake only that one subject test. Of course, since most people aren't thrilled about having to take any standardized test, this could be called "finding the silver lining in the cloud." Yet there's no need to feel bad if you do happen to get a low score, because high GHSGT scores are not very common.

> For each subject test, you'll receive a scaled score between 400–600. To pass, you must receive a score of 500 or higher.

How the GHSGT Tests Were Born

Currently, there are two different stories circulating about the origin of the GHSGT.

Version A:

Twenty years ago, on the coldest night of winter, a 100-pound meteor crashed into a peach orchard outside of Ochlocknee, Georgia. The meteor cracked open on impact, and at its core were the very first GHSGT tests.

Version B:

In 1991 the Georgia state assembly passed a law stating that high school students must pass a series of tests in order to receive a high school diploma. These were known as *Basic Skills Tests*. Several years later the Georgia Board of Education revised the state's learning standards. These new standards, called the *Quality Core Curriculum*, required an updated version of exams, which led to the creation of the GHSGT.

While on a stroll, an educator watches a batch of GHSGT tests fall to Earth.

While most people prefer version B because of its greater adherence to the facts, version A does have the advantage of making a better made-for-television movie.

Whichever story you prefer, the truth is that the GHSGT is here to stay, and that's why this book was written. If taking the GHSGT is like driving a car for the first time, then *Ultimate GHSGT* provides you with cool wheels, a great road map, the best insurance, and all the training you need to make the experience a successful one. We have included all the techniques and strategies you need to do well on each subject test, and we've also provided GHSGT-like sample questions throughout the book to help you practice these skills. If you study these strategies and apply them on the test, then taking the GHSGT should change from a difficult experience into something as easy as driving to the beach on the first day of summer break.

Chapter 1

TEST-TAKING STRATEGIES

HOW TEST-TAKING STRATEGIES ARE LIKE A SWISS ARMY KNIFE

This chapter will provide you with the test-taking strategies you'll need in order to succeed on the GHSGT. You might be using some of these techniques already, but there's a big difference between using test-taking strategies some of the time and using them all of the time, for every subject test.

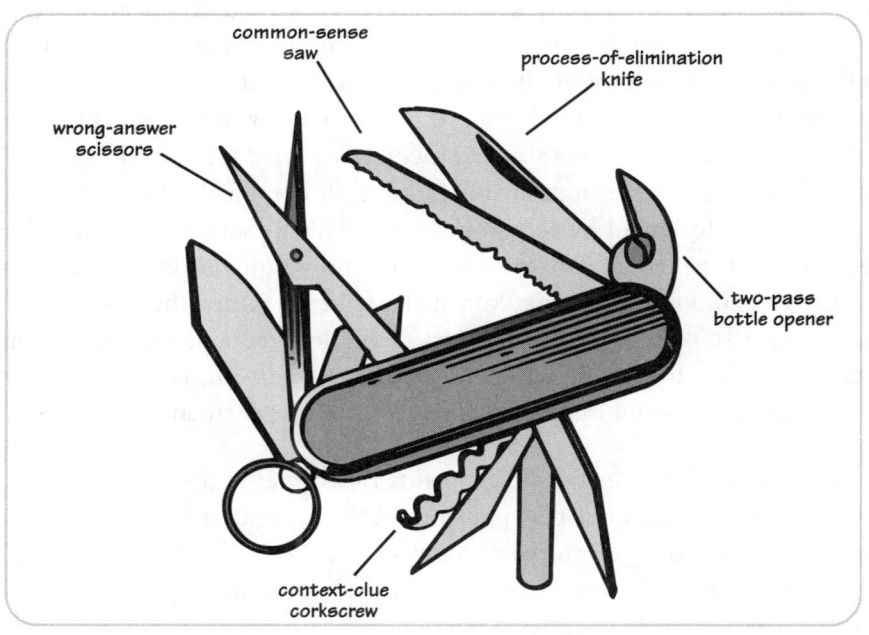

A multi-purpose test-taking tool

In this respect test-taking skills are like that Swiss Army knife you got for Christmas: If you look at it just once and then put it in a drawer, it will never help you. If you occasionally carry it around, you might find some use for it, but it's more likely you'll forget it's there and not use it when a situation arises. But if you take the knife and examine how all the different parts can be used, then you'll find you have the perfect tool for many different occasions.

This same premise holds true for the following test-taking strategies. If you take the time and practice using all of these techniques, you'll help yourself out on the GHSGT as well as on any other standardized tests you'll take in the future.

Strategy 1

Know the format of each GHSGT subject test *before* test day.

Make sure you know exactly many multiple-choice questions are on each subject test, and roughly how many questions you'll have to get right in order to pass (70 percent of all the questions is a good rule of thumb). This is important for two reasons. First, you need to know what to expect in order to prepare for it—you don't want to mentally prepare for a killer essay only to find out that the questions are all multiple-choice. Furthermore, knowing the format beforehand helps eliminate some of the anxiety you might be feeling about the test. If you know what questions you'll be facing, then you should feel empowered by that knowledge, since it means that the GHSGT won't surprise or upset you. However, if the test remains this mysterious exam you have to pass in order to graduate, you'll probably feel a little nervous about it—and that could affect your test performance.

In terms of the Swiss Army knife, knowing the format of the test is like using the little magnifying glass that pops out at the far end. It lets you examine the GHSGT up close so you can understand it better. The format of each subject test will be discussed later in the book, but for now you should familiarize yourself with the following facts:

1. The GHSGT is made up of five different tests.

There are four tests in content areas: English language arts, math, science, and social studies. The fifth test is a writing test.

2. The tests are given in timed sessions.

You will have three hours to finish each of the four content tests. You will have 90 minutes to complete the Writing test.

3. The Writing test is given in the fall of your junior year, and the four content tests in the spring.

The four content tests are given on different days within the same week.

4. With the exception of the Writing test, the four content tests are entirely multiple-choice.

Each content test contains the following number of questions.

English/Language Arts (ELA):   50 questions

Math: 60 questions

Science: 70 questions

Social Studies: 80 questions

Note: These numbers do not take into account an additional 10 *field-test questions* on each test. These are questions that the Department of Education is trying out for possible future use, and they do not count toward your score. There is no way to recognize them, however, so just work through the test normally and don't get worked up over any one question. In the end, that question might not count!

For the Writing test, you will be asked to write a persuasive essay on a given topic. The essay must be no longer than two pages.

Now that you know how many questions are on each exam, suppose you come to a really tough question on the ELA test. Should you spend ten minutes to make sure you get it right? The answer is, No.

Strategy 2

Don't spend too much time and energy on any one question at the expense of the other questions.

Although you have up to three hours to take each test (with the exception of the Writing test), this is not recommended. Mental fatigue will inevitably set in, as will sheer boredom. Each exam is designed to be completed in 60–90 minutes. While you should never rush a question in order to stay within the "recommended" time, keeping a good pace will help you to stay focused and to keep from getting mentally exhausted.

There are no trick questions on the test. Negatively worded questions and convoluted combinations of answers do not appear unless needed for clarification.

On most tests you take in high school, you try to get the highest grade possible, which means answering every question no matter how long it takes. This isn't a good idea here, because on the GHSGT, there are only two real grades: Pass or Fail. Spending too much time on any one question means you've wasted precious minutes and increased your mental fatigue greatly.

KAPLAN

An older Georgia students berates himself for taking too long on a question.

Strategy 3

Maintain a consistent pace throughout the test. Don't rush through—or spend too long on—any one question.

Proper pacing is something that all good test takers do naturally, but that can be learned quite easily by everyone else. Here are all the ingredients you'll need.

Mom's Old-Fashioned Pacing Recipe

Ingredients:

1. Two eyes (one eye will do as well).

2. A watch.
   A digital watch or stopwatch is preferable, since it provides a more accurate display. Sundials and grand-father clocks are not a good choice.

Directions:

Use ingredient 1 to look at ingredient 2. Repeat often so that you have an accu-rate idea of how many questions are left, and how much remaining time you have to work on them.

Granted, pacing sounds simple, but in the heat of the moment this is one strategy people often abandon first—and usually with negative results. Make sure you practice pacing before Test Day. In fact, you'll find that it will also help you in other parts of your life, as good time management skills are use-ful to have.

By setting—and keeping—a proper pace for yourself, and by going into the test knowing what you'll see, you'll be taking control of the test. In other words, go in with a game plan of how much time you'll want to spend on each question. This will be much better than just showing up and scribbling frantically once the exam begins.

Spend about 2 or 3 minutes on each multiple-choice question.

KAPLAN

Strategy 4

Do all the easy questions first before tackling the hard questions.

Many tests are arranged so that the easiest items are first and the hardest items are last. The GHSGT is not arranged that way, so it is possible to see several difficult questions in a row, for example, followed by some easier questions.

That said, go through and do the easy questions first, holding off on the hard questions for later. Why spend time on a hard question when there are easier questions, and easier points, waiting for you after it?

Strategy 5

Use a two-pass system on the test. On the first pass, answer the easy questions and skip the rest. Then go back a second time and answer the more challenging questions.

The best way to approach the test is to use a two-pass system, going through the test twice. The first time through, if you come to a question that stumps you, after a minute or two just move on. You can come back to it. Concentrate on answering the questions you know. The second pass is the time to attack the more difficult problems. If you're working at a consistent pace, you should more time on the second pass to work on the more challenging questions.

A farmer considers how to use the two-pass system on his crops.

Let's say you find yourself staring at a geometry question you have no idea how to solve. You look at it briefly on the first pass, but the question is very unfamiliar to you, so you move on to the remaining questions. On the second pass, you reread the problem, but it still doesn't make sense. Should you just skip it and move on? The answer is "Absolutely not!" There's no penalty for wrong answers on the test, so any question you leave blank is a missed opportunity for free points.

Strategy 6

Don't leave any questions blank. You won't lose points for wrong answers, so even if you have to guess, answer every question!

Some tests, like the SAT, deduct any wrong answers you make from your total score. But this isn't the case on the GHSGT: Your score is based only on the number of questions you answer correctly, so any question you leave blank is a missed opportunity for free points.

　1.　What is the proper motion of Barnard's star?*

　　A. 14 millibreems

　　B. 10.25 arc seconds a year

　　C. 6.12 star miles

　　D. The Treaty of Ghent

This question is impossibly hard, but if you guess, you still have a one-in-four chance of getting it right. If you do get it right, it won't matter that it was a guess; all that will matter is that the proper oval has been filled in. Of course it helps if you can rule out one or more answer choices before you guess. That way, you'll improve your odds of guessing correctly.

Strategy 7

Use the Process of Elimination to help you find the correct answer. Try ruling out clearly wrong answers one by one.

* The answer is B. This question is much tougher than an actual GHSGT question.

If test-taking strategies are like a Swiss Army knife, then the Process of Elimination (POE) is the biggest, strongest knife in the set. POE is something most students know about, but rarely use; they tend to rely instead solely on their knowledge of the subject. Knowing the answer to a question outright is great, but when that fails, POE is the most effective tool you can use to get the right answer anyway. On every multiple-choice question, the answer is in front of you. All that matters is whether or not you pick the correct answer. Look at the following two questions.

2. Who was the thirteenth president of the United States?
   Place your answer here. _____

3. Who was the thirteenth president of the United States?

   A. Abraham Lincoln

   B. Leo Tolstoy

   C. Millard Fillmore

   D. Chuckles the Clown

On question 2, if you don't know the answer, you have almost no chance of getting it right. But on question 3, you can use POE and eliminate any answer choices you think are wrong. D is out, and if there was ever a president named Tolstoy, you would have remembered it, so B must be out as well. That leaves A or C—at this point, it's a fifty-fifty shot, so take a guess and move on. You won't guess the right answer all the time, of course, but if you use POE regularly and effectively, you'll get enough questions right to boost your score.

Common sense is an important part of POE. In question 3, common sense told you that America would never elect a clown to be a president (though some U.S. historians would tell you that Warren G. Harding comes pretty close). Look at how common sense can help you eliminate some answer choices in the following math problem.

4. Feinberg Fabrics uses the following price list for its cotton sheets.

Area	Price
3 cm^2	$6.00
6 cm^2	$9.30
9 cm^2	$12.90
12 cm^2	$16.80

Based on this information, what would an 18 cm^2 sheet likely cost?

A. $12.00

B. $16.60

C. $18.60

D. $25.50

Before you start working out the math, use common sense and POE first. According to the chart, if a 12 cm^2 sheet costs $16.80, will a larger sheet (18 cm^2) cost more or less than that? A larger sheet will cost more, so the correct answer will have to be more than $16.80. Using POE then, you can eliminate A and B, since those answer choices are less than $16.80. That leaves C and D, and at this point, you can take an educated guess. Looking at the pricing chart, you might note how the price appears to jump by 3 or 4 dollars each time. Answer choice C is only 2 dollars greater than $16.80, so D would be a safer bet. And it's the right answer!

POE can be used on all the subject tests. Look back to question 1, the Barnard's star question. If you had to eliminate one answer choice, which one would it be? Well, choice D, The Treaty of Ghent, doesn't seem to have much to do with stars or motion, so it can be crossed out. This leaves you with a one-in-three chance of guessing correctly.

Strategy 8

If an answer choice looks too good to be true, it probably is. Remember that the test is designed to challenge you, so don't just jump at the first answer choice that you suspect is right.

Even if you see an answer choice that "looks right" in 15 seconds, try to resist the urge to select it and move on. In order to make these questions challenging to students, the test makers throw in tempting wrong answer choices. These "attractive but wrong" answer choices might apply the right information in the wrong way, or they might include irrelevant details. Don't be misled! Read the question carefully to make sure you are answering the question that is asked, using the full recommended 2 or 3 minutes to consider all the answer choices. Let's look at question 3 again.

3. Who was the thirteenth president of the United States?

A. Abraham Lincoln

B. Leo Tolstoy

C. Millard Fillmore

D. Chuckles the Clown

Look back at question 1. Does any answer choice look too good to be true? Since the word *star* appears in the question and in answer choice C, it's unlikely that C is correct–that would be too easy! And as it turns out, the answer is B.

Of these four names, almost everybody will recognize one president: Abraham Lincoln. If you were in a hurry, this question would take 15 seconds, since you would likely pick the first (and perhaps only) name you recognized. But if you understand how the GHSGT works, and how best to approach a standardized test, you won't make that mistake. Using POE, you could eliminate B and D, as you did earlier. That leaves A and C, and frankly, choice A, Abraham Lincoln, is just too good to be true. That leaves C, so Millard Fillmore must have been the thirteenth president.

Since multiple-choice questions comprise four out of the five tests, using POE consistently can be a great boon to your score. Throughout this book, be sure you test your POE skills on every multiple-choice question you work on.

Strategy 9

Take short breaks during the test to help you relieve mental fatigue.

If you feel yourself getting mentally tired during the test, just put your pencil down and take a minute to stretch. Stretch your arms, stretch your fingers, clear your mind, and then refocus your thoughts back on the test. Sometimes you have to *take* time to *save* time!

Strategy 10

Be of sound (and well-rested) mind and body for the test.

All the studying and practice you do for the GHSGT could be lost if you show up on test day cranky, tired, and hungry. Getting a good night's sleep and having a healthy breakfast are essential for a good test performance. It's hard to concentrate on a test when your stomach is grumbling so loud it sounds like Mozart's *Requiem Mass* is being performed in your duodenum. Make sure you eat a good breakfast, but don't eat so heavily that you find yourself dying for a nap. A bowl of cereal, toast, and fruit is a good way to start the day. If your school allows it, bring along an easy-to-eat snack.

In addition to a nutritious meal, a good night's rest is vital to having a clear head on test day. This means no cramming! Staying

A positive attitude on test day is worth more than any single fact you might study the night before the exam.

up late into the night studying for the test is not a good idea, since that will tire you out and is bound to increase your stress level.

Do your studying ahead of time. That way, your confidence will be highest right before the test. If you do want to review some things on the day before the test, go over more general items, such as the test format and general test-taking strategies. This will help you more than cramming on subject matter.

Instead of studying on the night before the test, you're better off doing something that relaxes you and takes your mind off the exam. Don't exhaust yourself physically—no extreme sports! Play a board game or watch a video. If you like, a short walk or a quick hike in a nearby park is also a good idea. But remember, if you do go on a hike, be sure to bring along your Swiss Army knife and use it in as many ways as possible.

Strategy Review

Strategy 1:   Know the format of each GHSGT subject test before test day.

Strategy 2:   Don't spend too much time and energy on any one question at the expense of the other questions.

Strategy 3:   Maintain a consistent pace throughout the test. Don't rush through—or spend too long on—any one question.

Strategy 4:   Do all the easy questions first before tackling the hard questions.

Strategy 5:   Use a two-pass system on the test. On the first pass, answer the easy questions and skip the rest. Then go back a second time and answer the more challenging questions.

Strategy 6:   Don't leave any questions blank. You won't lose points for wrong answers, so even if you have to guess, answer every question!

Strategy 7:   Use the Process of Elimination to help you find the correct answer. Try ruling out clearly wrong answers one by one.

Strategy 8:   If an answer choice looks too good to be true, it probably is. Remember that the test is designed to challenge you, so don't just jump at the first answer choice that you suspect is right.

Strategy 9:   Take short breaks during the test to help you relieve mental fatigue.

Strategy 10:   Be of sound (and well-rested) mind and body for the test.

Chapter 2

WRITING

HOW THE GHSGT WRITING PROMPT IS LIKE A STICK OF BUBBLE GUM

By itself, a stick of bubble gum is not very interesting. It's nothing more than a flat, strangely colored rectangle made out of a substance that looks a lot like cardboard. But once you place the gum in your mouth, everything starts to change. First, you get a burst of flavor, and as your jaw muscles start flexing, the gum takes on an ever-changing variety of shapes. Place the gum between your lips, exhale, and the flat stick of gum has transformed into a bubble-gum bubble.

Similarly, the GHSGT writing prompt is nothing more than a string of words. It's up to you to take the prompt and use it to create a concise, insightful essay that will earn you a high score. To do this you'll have to read the prompt, flex your mental muscles to come up with the key ingredients for your composition, and then exhale those words onto paper. The end result should be an essay that is as contained and logical as a sphere of chewing gum.

Although you're probably well-versed in the basics of essay writing, this chapter will review what's expected of you on the Writing test.

> Officially, the Writing test is called the *Georgia High School Writing Test* (GHSWT).

While the four multiple-choice content area tests are given to juniors in the spring semester, the Writing test is given in the fall. Since it is the first test you will encounter, it is discussed first in this book.

A solitary student walks the moors preparing for the GHSGT essay.

Format of the Writing GHSGT

Quite simply, the Writing test gives you 90 minutes to write an essay on a specified topic. On the day of the test, the schedule should run as follows:

1. Students arrive and sit down in desks.
2. Students plead with administrator in charge to get out of taking the test.
3. Administrator either

    a) says "no"; or

    b) does not dignify statement with a response.
4. Students receive a writing prompt (assignment/instructions) for a persuasive essay.
5. Students now have 90 minutes in which to write their essays.

KAPLAN

Scoring

Your essay will be graded by two readers, each of whom will judge it on the following four qualities.

Writing Test Domains	What it Means
1. *Content/Organization*	Is there a coherent structure to the essay, with a beginning, middle, and end? Are there sufficient details and illustrations? Are they relevant and clearly developed? Are there logical transitions and a flow of ideas?
2. *Style*	Is the tone consistent with the topic and purpose? Is effective diction used? Is there varied sentence structure?
3. *Conventions of Written Language*	Does the essay use proper grammar usage, punctuation, and spelling?
4. *Sentence Formation*	Are there complete sentences? Is there appropriate use of end punctuation?

As you can see, there are four things the graders will look for in your essay, though they are not equally weighted. In fact, the first category, *Content/Organization*, accounts for twice as much as the other three categories. So if you write a moving, well-developed essay with atrocious grammar, you might still score well. But if you write a bland, undeveloped essay with perfect grammar, you might not do so well. Since *Content/Organization* counts for more than the other domains, that's your first priority.

Strategy

When developing your essay, concentrate *more* on the content and *less* on the grammar.

With this in mind, focus more on making your argument persuasive and concise rather than on using perfect grammar. You can always go through your essay before time runs out to check your spelling and grammar or to rewrite some sentences. However, if you write an unconvincing essay from the start, you're sure to be on the path to a lower score.

Make sure your essay:

• Responds to the assigned task

• Clearly establishes a main idea

• Presents relevant supporting examples

While content is more important than grammar here, your essay still has to be comprehensible. A sentence so jumbled that it barely makes sense won't help you, since the reader won't understand the point you are trying to make. Consider the following three sentences.

A. I believe students should be allowed to vote in national elections.

B. I beleive the students they should be aloud to vote national elections.

C. I believe the students they vote and national elections.

Version A has proper grammar and clear content. Version B has some misspellings and incorrect grammar, but the writer still makes his point. Version C, however, is grammatically incorrect and unclear. Shoot to write a "version A," and try your best to avoid writing a "version C."

Writing Prompt

The Writing test will start by presenting you with a persuasive prompt; that is, a statement or a topic. Your task will be to write an essay that persuades the reader of a certain point of view about that topic. For instance:

Persuasive Prompt Example

- Many adults think that having a curfew helps prevent crime. Write an essay on whether or not you believe a curfew effectively deters crime.

Time to Flex Your Mental Muscles

After reading the prompt, you should have around 43.7692 minutes left in the planning session. That's a lot of time, so don't feel pressured to start writing immediately.

Strategy

Give yourself about 10–15 minutes to brainstorm as many thoughts as possible. Write them all down.

The key to successful brainstorming is to draw some conclusions of your own, using the text to back up your ideas. Look at the sample writing prompt above again.

First, you have to decide what position you want to take on this subject. It doesn't matter what side of the argument you take; all that matters is how well you support your argument. There's no correct answer, only a well-supported argument versus a poorly supported argument.

Once you read the prompt, decide which side of the argument you want to support, and then start planning your essay.

Let's say you're going to write a persuasive essay which states that curfews are an effective deterrent to crime. Take some time right now to brainstorm as many ideas as possible that will help support this statement. Do this on your own, using separate paper, and then compare your list to the one below:

Procurfew Essay: Brainstorming Ideas

1. Most crimes occur at night: Having a curfew will limit a criminal's ability to get around.

2. Random crimes of opportunity, like breaking a car window to get to some CD's, should decrease.

3. Police will have an easier time preventing crime.

4. Infringement on people's freedom wouldn't be total—still a lot of time to roam streets.

5. A one-year study could be done to see if curfew is an effective deterrent.

6. Human-eating robots come out most often at night—curfew will help prevent crimes of digestion.

As you can see from item 6, some ideas aren't as good as others. Don't sweat it: The whole point of brainstorming is to come up with as many ideas as possible, even if you don't use them all. In fact, not all ideas will fit into your essay. Don't feel obligated to use an idea if it doesn't fit smoothly in your essay. It's better to elaborate on a few good ideas than just list a whole bunch of items that are weakly explored.

You'll have 90 minutes in which to complete the essay, but try not to drag out your time. Your essay must be up to two pages, which isn't a lot of space. If you do finish in less than 90 minutes, don't just add filler. Use that time to do a thorough review of your work. Correct and smooth out your sentence structure, transitions, and grammar, and then, hand it in! Look at the pacing suggestions below to get a sense of how to spend your time.

Pacing Suggestions

Read prompt & brainstorm	10 minutes
Plan and organize	15 minutes
Write essay	20 minutes
Edit/rewrite/proofread	10 minutes

After you finish brainstorming, take some time to organize your thoughts. Try writing out an informal outline to ensure that you have included all the major elements. Decide which ideas you'll use, what order they should go in, and how you'll transition all of them. Transitions are important in essay development; it's up to you, not the reader, to link your ideas together. Are these ideas similar? If so, how? Do they conflict? How?

> Your essay can be no more than two pages, so you'll have to write efficiently!

To return to the bubble gum analogy, if brainstorming is where you chew the gum, then organizing the essay is where you line up the gum between your lips in order to make the bubble. It's an important stage: If you place the gum in the wrong place, your bubble will pop before it ever gets big. If you don't organize your thoughts well, your essay never reaches the level of detail and clarity needed to get a high score.

Details, Details, Details

Precise, elaborate details are crucial to any essay. To illustrate their importance, read the following xsentences which range from *vague* to *elaborately detailed*. As you can see, providing sufficient details can mean the different between staying alive and becoming tiger chow.

1. There is a cat.

2. There is a large cat over there.

3. There is a large cat coming toward you.

4. There is a tiger running at you.

5. There is a vicious, five-hundred pound tiger running rapidly toward you!

Luckily, the GHSGT is not so high-stakes that you have to write a perfectly composed and compelling essay. However, you should make it a point to elaborate on all of your ideas, clarifying their meanings as well as possible. For instance, look at the following statement.

> Random crimes of opportunity, like breaking a car window to get to some CD's, should decrease.

This statement is far too incomplete. To correct it, add something like this:

> With a curfew, many random crimes of opportunity should decrease. Many times teenagers, who commit a fair amount of vandalism and petty theft, are simply bored. They walk around the neighborhood looking for something to do, and often end up doing something foolish and criminal—like breaking a car window to get to some CD's—just for a thrill. However, with a curfew in place, the opportunity to commit random crimes would decrease, since teenagers would not be as likely to go out, and if they did, they would have to be much more cautious in their activities. While an increase in bored teenagers indoors might lead to an increase in prank phone calls, at least property damage should decrease. And, these days, there's always caller identification!

The response above takes the original idea and elaborates on its meaning. The more of this you can do, the more persuasive your argument will be, giving your essay score a boost.

The Opposing Argument

When writing a persuasive essay, don't forget that there's always another valid viewpoint on the subject. The fact that you chose the procurfew side doesn't mean that the anticurfew side is completely wrong. So put away your procurfew posters, cancel the procurfew rally you planned, and take some time to think about what reasons would validate the anticurfew argument. Include one or two of those reasons in your own essay, explaining why you disagree.

Strategy

Try to present an understanding of *both* sides of an argument. If you can describe the other side's position, and reasons why you disagree with it, then you have strengthened your essay.

Looking at the list of brainstorming ideas, you will see that in items 4 and 5, there's an attempt to see the anticurfew side of things, and a subsequent attempt to counter those arguments. That portion of your essay could look something like this:

> Many people would argue that a curfew is unconstitutional because it infringes on their freedom. While this is a valid concern, there are steps that could be taken to limit this argument. First, the curfew could be set late at night— say, from midnight to 6:00 A.M—so that the majority of the population wouldn't even notice, or mind, its existence. While this type of late curfew would prevent insomniacs from taking a stroll at 3:00 A.M., it would also help protect the community. As a whole, everyone would benefit. Besides, the insomniacs in question would have 18 other hours in the day to walk, not an unreasonable amount of time. Second, the curfew could be a temporary one, say for one year, to judge how effectively it deters crime. If it is not effective, or if it deters only a small percentage of

> crime, then it could be abandoned. But if the curfew leads
> to a significant decrease in criminal activity, which is very
> possible, then most people would probably want to keep it
> in place.

The paragraph above acknowledges the opposition's argument and counters it. While you shouldn't spend the entire essay attacking your opponent's position, one paragraph on the subject is an excellent idea.

Hey Mumbles! Be Sure to Write Neatly

If your cursive handwriting is so bad that sometimes even you don't understand it, make sure you print out your essay. An illegible essay cannot be graded, and it would be a tragedy if a well-written essay lost points simply because the graders—who have to read a lot of essays, mind you—could not read what you have written. Even a partially illegible essay may suffer at score time.

Once you finish writing your essay, make sure to take some time to proofread for mistakes. Rewrite any awkward sentences. Make sure you have used transitions correctly. Your essay should be smooth and concise.

Strategy

Make sure you proofread your essay and correct any errors in grammar, punctuation, or sentence construction. Make all corrections neatly.

Once you have finished checking your essay, you're done! Now that the Writing test is under your belt, you have some time off before the other subject tests are given. There's nothing to do but kick back, relax, and maybe . . . chew some gum.

Chapter 3

ENGLISH/LANGUAGE ARTS

HOW ANSWERING ELA QUESTIONS IS LIKE COMING UP WITH SEVEN SYNONYMS FOR *SQUEAL*

From memory, can you come up with seven words that mean the same thing as *squeal*? *Cry* is a good choice, and so are *scream* and *yell*. *Shriek* makes four synonyms, and after that . . . well, there's always *grumpy*, *sneezy*, and *bashful*. Wait—those last three are Seven Dwarves, not seven synonyms.

Coming up with seven definitions for *squeal* at the drop of a hat isn't easy. What if you were asked the same question, yet this time you could use a thesaurus to help you? Since a thesaurus is a reference book devoted to synonyms, the task becomes much easier: Just thumb through it until you reach *squeal*, and look at all the synonyms. You'll find *cry, scream, yell, shriek, wail, yelp,* and *whine*, not to mention *shrill, screech, peep, bawl,* and *squeak*.

It's obviously easier to refer to the thesaurus than to use just your memory. The same holds true for the passages on the English/Language Arts (ELA) test. It's in your best interest to look back at a passage for an answer. Even so, many students will read a passage and then try to answer the

Some questions, like analogies questions, are not accompanied by a passage. For these, keep in mind:

1. You can still use Process of Elimination.

2. A difficult question for you is most likely difficult for everyone.

3. One question will not make or break your score.

questions from memory. It's like struggling to come up with seven synonyms for *squeal* when you have a thesaurus sitting in front of you: It is not the most effective approach.

On this part of the test, you need to treat all the reading passages like the thesaurus, and continuously refer to them.

Strategy

The answer to a reading passage question lies somewhere in the passage itself, and that's where you should always look.

Some students might resist looking back at a passage, as it seems to be a waste of time. They might argue, "Why should I look back? The answer is right in front of me in the form of answer choices!" While that's true, it's also true that there are several wrong answer choices in front of you. Furthermore, it's not always so clear that those wrong answer choices are wrong. In fact, most wrong answer choices are designed to trip you up if you don't consider them carefully, so it's always worth your while to refer to the text.

© 2000 PhotoSpin Inc.

Trying to answer GHSGT Reading questions without referring to the passage can lead you into a big hole.

KAPLAN

ELA Test Facts

The English/Language Arts test contains 50 questions (plus an additional 10 field-test questions), broken down into three content categories.

Content	Percentage of Test
1. Reading/Literature	47–49%
2. Critical Thinking	37–39%
3. Writing/Usage Grammar	14–16%

Many of the ELA questions involve short articles, poems, and passages from reference or historical documents. Because these passages vary in length, you can't assign a specific amount of reading time to all the passages. You can't say, "I'll spend two minutes reading each passage," since that would leave you rushing through the 200-word passage and wasting time on the 40-word passage. There are no hard-and-fast pacing rules to guide you here. Having said that, there are certain things you should keep in mind.

Rather than focus on the specific content areas of the test, this book focuses on general test-taking strategies that can be applied across the board to all question types.

Strategy

Read to *understand*, not to *memorize*, each passage. Don't get stuck poring over the text, even if it's fascinating. Your task here is to answer questions and move on.

As you work through a text, read with an eye toward overall comprehension, not toward memorization. It's more important to understand the main idea and overall development of a passage than it is to memorize details. What is the main idea? What is the tone of the passage? the author's point of view?

Then, focus in on where supporting storylines and details are located—for instance, paragraph 2 deals with snakes, while paragraph 3 is about ladders. Then, head to the questions. That way, if the first question is a main idea question, you'll be in good shape answering it, and if the next question asks about ladders, you'll know where to look—in paragraph 3, since it deals with ladders.

By reading for the main idea/text development first, and for the details second, you'll be able to head right to the section of text that you need to answer a question. To help you do this, as you read the passage the first time, jot down notes and your own personal reminders. They don't need to be intricate, precise sentences about what occurs in each paragraph, but they should act as markers to remind you about what's in each part of the passage. These markers should help you answer questions faster, and answering questions is what the ELA test is all about.

Certain types of questions are common on reading tests, and knowing about them ahead of time will help you on Test Day. Before reviewing them, however, read the following sample passage. Remember to keep your eye on understanding the passage, not on memorizing it.

The following excerpt has been adapted from Act I, Scene 2 from The Duchess of Malfi *by John Webster, published in 1623.*

Delio: Then the law to the duke
Is like a foul black cobweb to a spider,
He makes it his dwelling and a prison
To entangle those shall feed him.

Antonio: Most true: [5]
He never pays debts unless they be shrewd turns,
And those he will confess that he doth owe.
Last, for his brother there, the cardinal,
They that do flatter him most say oracles
Hang at his lips; and truly I believe them,   [10]
For the darkness speaks in them.
But for their sister, the right noble duchess,
You never fix'd your eye on three fair medals,

Cast in one figure, of so different temper.
For her discourse, it is so full of rapture,   [15]
You only will begin then to be sorry
When she does end her speech, and wish, in wonder,
She held it less vain-glory, to talk much,
Than your penance to hear her: while she speaks,
She throws upon a man so sweet a look,   [20]
That it were able to raise one to a dance
That lay in a dead palsy.

. . .

Delio: Fie, Antonio,
You play yourself out with her commendation.

Antonio: I'll case the picture up, only thus much,   [25]
All her particular worth grows to this sum;
She stains the time past: lights the time to come.

The Big Five Question Types

If the GHSGT were an *un*-standardized test, a book like this would be impossible to write. One year the test might be all essays, the next year it might consist of just fill-in-the-blank questions, and the after year that it might be nothing more than a teacher standing in front of you asking, "Guess what number I'm thinking of now?"

Fortunately, the GHSGT is a standardized test, so the question types remain fairly consistent from year to year. On the ELA test, there are five basic types of multiple-choice question, so we'll call them the *Big Five*. Of course, there are bound to be some questions that don't fall neatly into one of these categories, so be prepared for that. Also, the question types can change slightly from year to year. That said, by familiarizing yourself with the *Big Five*, you'll be able to learn techniques and strategies that will help you on all question types.

Process of Elimination on the Reading Passages

The reading passages on the ELA test have been chosen or written by educators. Since this is the case, you'll never see an essay on how to win at gambling or a poem about robbing banks. Instead, you'll read passages that are informative and educational, and that strive to make a positive point. With this in mind, eliminate any answer choices that are too extreme or negative. Look instead for answer choices that are more general, somewhat positive, and easier to prove.

Strategy

As a general rule, when using POE on the reading passages, answer choices that are too extreme or negative are unlikely to be correct. Look for an answer that is broad, somewhat positive, and easier to prove.

1. What concept about Julius and Garcon is most thoroughly developed in the passage?

   A. Both men came from wealthy families.

   B. The two men had nothing at all in common.

   C. The two men represented different cultures.

   D. Julius and Garcon hated each other.

 Even though you know nothing about the passage, you can cross out answer choices that are too extreme or negative. What would you eliminate? Choice B is rather extreme; if the two men had just one thing in common, it's incorrect, so it can go. D is pretty harsh, and while there's a slim chance it's true, your best bet is to cross it out. That leaves A and C, which gives you a fifty-fifty shot for guessing, and you never even saw the passage.

2. What is the best inference that can be made from the Governor's statement?

   A. There was some confusion after the hurricane.

   B. People were scared to go to the disaster shelters.

   C. Most people were robbing stores downtown.

   D. Absolute panic had broken out throughout the city.

Here, C isn't a good choice because it uses the word *most*—this implies a majority of people. In order for that to be correct, the passage would have had to state that 51 percent or more of the people were robbing, and this seems extreme and too negative for the GHSGT. Choice D has the same problem, with the word *absolute*. What if some people were only half-panicked? There goes your *absolute*. Choice D also isn't very positive. That leaves A and B.

Choice A might work because it has the bland word *some* in it. *Some* can mean *a little*, or it could mean *a lot*, but it's fairly vague and therefore easy to prove. If just one person is confused, that means there's *some* confusion. As for B, a dose of common sense will cast this answer choice into a bad light. Why would people be afraid to seek a disaster shelter after a hurricane? That makes little sense. Of course, there's a chance that B is correct, but A is by far your best bet using POE. And guess what? It's the correct answer.

The Big Five Multiple Choice Question Types

As you analyze the following question types, keep in mind the following question: "Are there any answer chances that can be eliminated using POE?" If you practice POE until it becomes second nature, your test performance is sure to improve. If you simply read about it now, but never use it again, it will be of minimal benefit.

1. Vocabulary Questions

The first category is the vocabulary question. These questions ask, in some form or another, "What does _____ mean?" To answer these correctly, you'll need to either:

      A. Know the definition of the word already; or
      B. Figure out the meaning of the word from the words around it.

Option A is just nifty, but Option B is a test-taking skill that's useful to know, so that's what we'll focus on. Option B, also called *learning in context*, is something everyone can do. Look at the question below.

3 Joan said, "Please get the *sargfrommanhemmar* from the fridge and serve some to our guests, who are no doubt very hungry." What does *sargfrommanhemmar* mean?

A. It is a type of food.

B. It is a highly venomous sea snake.

C. It is a type of drink.

D. It is a statue made out of clay.

Based on Joan's sentence, which answer would you choose? If you choose A, you would be right. (If you choose B, you probably don't have many guests still living.) Using the words around *sargfrommanhemmar*, you can deduce that it's a type of food, which is why it was in the "fridge." Choice C is a close second guess, but why would you give a drink to people who are "hungry"? If the word *hungry* were replaced with *thirsty* in the original sentence, C would be a better answer.

After a day of testing, the locals relax and enjoy a bowl of sargfrommanhemmar at Jakob's Backway Eatery.

KAPLAN

Strategy

On Vocabulary Questions, read the sentences around the unknown word to figure out its meaning.

Try the following question, making sure to check back to the *Duchess of Malfi* passage on page 34.

4. In line 22, what does the word *palsy* mean?
   A. eager to dance

   B. prepared to fight

   C. ready to flee

   D. unable to move

To answer this question, don't read simply the line that has *palsy* in it; always start two or three lines earlier and read through to the sentence that follows. Since you have already read through the passage for its main idea, you hopefully have the idea that "the Duchess is really beautiful, wonderful woman," or something along those lines. With this as your framework, looking over lines 20–22 you should realize that she is so beautiful and kind, she could make someone dance who was . . . *unable to move*, choice D.

Another approach here would be to use Elimination. Some wrong answer choices are meant to mislead or distract you (thus, their name *distractors*), so be careful not to rush through seemingly easy questions. For example, in question 4, choice A has the word *dance* in it; since the line just before line 22 has the word *dance* in it, you might incorrectly be tempted to choose it. Cross it out instead. Then, using common sense, you might notice that line 22 actually says *dead palsy*, and this makes B and C unlikely answer choices. How could somebody be *dead* and *prepared to fight or flee* at the same time? You can be *dead* and *unable to move*, however.

2. Main Idea/Passage Formation Questions

These questions test your understanding of a passage's main idea. Sometimes they're straightforward, but oftentimes, they're not.

5. Which of the following statements best describes the passage?

   A. The Duchess is a good person, but her brothers are not.

   B. The Duke and the Cardinal are completely evil.

   C. Most people love the Duchess more than the Duke.

   D. The Duke rarely pays his debts.

6. Identify the section of the passage that discusses the Duke only.

   A. Lines 5–7

   B. Lines 8–11

   C. Lines 5–11

   D. Lines 8–11

Question 5 is a fairly straightforward Main Idea question, while Question 6 asks for something more precise. In other words, while questions 5 wants to know about the whole reading, question 6 asks if you grasped the outline of a section in the passage.

Strategy

On Main Idea/Passage Formation questions, look for answer choices that state the big picture and eliminate answer choices that are too small in scope.

To understand this strategy, look at question 5: Compare choices A and D. Both statements are true, though D is simply one small fact. Choice A is a broader statement that covers the entire reading. Specific facts from the passage might very well be included as misleading answer choices: These facts are usually accurate—they just don't represent the main idea of the text. Choice B is too extreme, since "completely evil" is impossible to prove— what if the Cardinal liked helping lost puppies, and the Duke was devoted to preserving the rainforest? That would mean they're not completely evil, though from what is read, they're pretty bad.

Choice C represents another type of wrong answer choice commonly seen on Main Idea questions: the *probably true* statement. From what you can infer from the text, chances are that you think the Duchess is a likeable person, but where is that stated in the passage? The answer: Nowhere. This is why referring to the passage is always a good idea. If you suspected choice C was right, you'd have to be able to back it up—but nowhere do the characters mention that the citizens of Malfi love the Duchess more than the Duke. So while there's a good chance that that's true, you cannot safely conclude that.

Question 6 might be easy if you had jotted down notes to yourself as you read the passage. You might have written "Duke = bad," "Cardinal = evil," and "Duchess = kind, pretty" in the margin of the text. If you did, then you're in good shape, but if not, it's just a matter of referring to the passage to see when Antonio talks about the Duke. Lines 5–7 describe the Duke, while line 8 starts a description of the Duke's brother, the Cardinal. Since the question asks about "the Duke only," A is the correct response.

3. Literary Terms Questions

Do you know the difference between a stalactite and a stalagmite? Good for you, but it won't help on the test. What will help you is if you know the difference between a *simile* and *irony*, since you'll be asked about literary terms.

Strategy

Make sure you know the definitions for the following literary terms:

* Simile	* Alliteration	* Metaphor
* Irony	* Hyperbole	* Personification
* Oxymoron		

Literary Terms Question are fairly simple—if you know the terms. If you don't know the terms, you'll have to guess, leaving you with a one-in-four chance of getting a question right. Before Test Day, make sure you learn what these terms mean. It's also a good idea to memorize examples of each. A GHSGT question may include other kinds of terms, but since the Reading/Literature strand makes up *almost half* of the test, chances are that a literary term will be the correct answer. As such, learn these terms first and worry about what *onomatopoeia* means at another time in your life.

7. Antonio states that the Duke, Duchess, and Cardinal are "three fair medals/Cast in one figure, of so different temper." This phrase is an example of

    A. irony.

    B. metaphor.

    C. simile.

    D. hyperbole.

8. Delio says "Then the law to the duke/Is like a foul black cobweb to a spider" . . . This phrase is an example of

    A. personification.

    B. metaphor.

    C. alliteration.

    D. simile.

Know the literary terms, and you'll know the right answers, B and D respectively.

KAPLAN

A wheel that talks is an extreme example of personification.

4. Inference Questions

A broad question category, Inference Questions are simply questions whose answers are not stated directly in the passage. Instead, the answer must be inferred from the text. For instance, although the *Duchess of Malfi* passage never exactly states the Cardinal is evil, you can infer this from the phrase, "the darkness speaks in them."

In some ways, Inference Question are like Vocabulary Questions, for which you must find clues that will help you define an unknown word. For Inference Questions, you also need to find clues that will help you draw conclusions and then answer the question.

9. According to Antonio, how did most people react when the Duchess stopped talking?

   A. They were disappointed.

   B. They were angry.

   C. They wanted to dance.

   D. They were struck by love.

Using POE, you can eliminate some choices before you refer to the passage for the answer. Since you know that the Duchess was a good person from your first read-through, B is an unlikely choice. Choice C takes the word *dance* directly from the passage, but from a reference Antonio makes about the Duchess's *looks*, not her *speech*. About her speech, Antonio states "You only will begin, then, to be sorry/When she doth end her speech." This is the clue that should lead you to choice A: *disappointed* is close to *sorry*. Again, since the answer is not actually spelled out in the passage, you'll have to read between the lines and select the closest answer choice.

Strategy

On Inference Questions, find the clues in the passage that will help you determine the answer. Since it won't be spelled out in the text, you'll have to infer the answer.

5. Emotion Questions

Rounding out the *Big Five* question types are Emotion Questions, which ask about the emotional state of the author or a character in the passage. In a way, these are a type of Inference Question, since you have to infer something (an emotional state) from clues in the text. Since the GHSGT is written by educators, a good fallback position on these questions is to look for a broad and positive answer, and then pick it.

Strategy

On Emotion Questions, the answer is unlikely to be extreme or very negative. Look instead for a broad answer that communicates something positive and educational.

KAPLAN

10. What emotion does Antonio appear to feel about the Duchess?

   A. friendship

   B. hatred

   C. mistrust

   D. admiration

11. Which word best describes the Duke's character?

   A. nurturing

   B. petty

   C. devious

   D. pious

Question 10 shows how you can sometimes get an answer without even looking at a passage. Choices B and C, *hatred* and *mistrust*, are both negative, so they're unlikely to be correct. That leaves A and D, and while it's a bit of a toss-up in terms of positivity, D is the right answer.

Question 11 shows that it always helps to check your answers by looking back at the reading. As useful as the "choose a broad and positive answer choice" strategy is, you can't apply it in every case. If you hadn't read the passage for this question, you might want to guess between A and D, both positive attributes. But since the Duke is a bad man, having been compared to "a foul black cobweb to a spider" (line 2), that won't work here. The answer is B or C, and from the spider comment you'll hopefully infer that *devious* is a better choice than merely *petty*.

Those are the *Big Five* questions types. Study the strategies for them, and practice as much as possible. Once you have finished taking the ELA exam, go outside, and then let out a squeal of delight. Or if you prefer, a *scream* of delight. Or a *yell, shriek, wail, yelp, whine, screech. . .*

Chapter 4

MATH

HOW DOING GHSGT MATH IS LIKE WATCHING *BAYWATCH* IN NEPAL

Landlocked between India and Tibet and home to nine of the world's ten largest mountains, Nepal doesn't get a lot of sun 'n' surf. This could explain why many Nepalis find *Baywatch* such an interesting program, as it takes place in an area of the world that's very sunny and definitely non-Himalayan.

If you were to hang out in Kathmandu, Nepal's capital, you might catch an episode or two of the show. At first glance, the Nepali *Baywatch* would probably confuse you, since the characters would be speaking a language you're unfamiliar with. Yet once you got over your initial confusion, you would see that the show really isn't hard to follow—even in Nepalese. A lifeguard's job is to save drowning people, and this is true regardless of what language is being spoken. Watching *Baywatch* in Nepal is just like watching *Baywatch* in Georgia—the characters still act the same way . . . if you call what they do "acting."

When you take the Math GHSGT, you might come across a question so confusing that it looks like Nepalese. If you let it rattle your nerves, chances are you'll lose confidence in your ability to solve it. But if you let your initial puzzlement pass, you should be able to figure out what the question is really asking. This is still a math test, and a fraction question is still a fraction question, regardless of how it appears. Many students can't get past their anxiety in these situations, and their scores inevitably suffer. If you go into the test knowing that a few questions will appear Nepalese to you, you'll be able to refocus your thoughts with confidence and figure out what's being asked of you.

> ### Strategy
>
> Some questions may look strange, but if you take the time to figure out what they're asking, then doing well on them should be as easy as spending the day at the beach.

Math Test Facts

The Math test includes 60 questions (plus an additional 10 field-test questions), broken down into three content categories.

Content	Percentage of Test
1. Number & Computation	17–19%
2. Data Analysis	19–21%
3. Measurement and Geometry	32–34%
4. Algebra	28–30%

Why You Don't Need to Memorize $\frac{4}{3}\pi^3$

You may have already spent a lot of energy trying to memorize formulas like the one above (which is the formula for the volume of a sphere). For this test, such memorization is not crucial; that's because your test booklet will include a math formula sheet with common algebra and geometry formulas. The test makers aren't testing your ability to memorize these formulas per se. They're more interested in how you apply the information. So focus more on learning how to work with the formulas than on memorizing them.

1. If a rectangular prism has a volume of 896 cubic feet, and its length and width are each 8 feet, what is its height? *(Use V = lwh)*

   A. 8 feet

   B. 12 feet

   C. 14 feet

   D. 16 feet

Strategy

To avoid making calculation errors, write *all* of your work down on paper. Always. And when using a calculator, write out every equation before punching in the numbers.

Writing out your work on paper is useful because it gives you something to examine when you're checking your answers. If you've merely punched in numbers on a calculator, there's no way to catch a mistake! Many math problems require more than one step of work, which increases your odds of making errors. Do all your calculations on paper, even if it takes a bit longer to finish. You'll be glad later that you took the extra time to do so.

Calculators are permitted on the test. But *before* you start punching in numbers, make sure to write out all your calculations on paper.

For question 1, having the formula sheet will help you immensely. First, write out the formula for the volume of a rectangular prism (also known as a *box*).

$$V = l \times w \times h$$

Then substitute the numbers that you know:

$$896 = 8 \times 8 \times h$$
$$896 = 64 \times h$$
$$\frac{896}{64} = h$$
$$14 = h$$

The answer is C.

Well-known formulas include the areas of squares, rectangles, circles, triangles, and trapezoids. Perimeter and circumference formulas may also appear on the test. Another important formula is the Pythagorean theorem, which allows you find the length of the third side of a right triangle if you know the other two sides.

Unable to use the Formula Sheet, a woman stands at her doorway hoping that someone will give her the formula 2(lw) + 2 (hw) + 2(lh).

Process of Elimination in Math

Imagine that on the Math test, the Process of Elimination was a kind of animal that had two dominant species:

> **Species 1:** *Numeralis eliminatorius*
> This form of elimination allows you to rule out answer choices that contain the same numbers used in the question.

> **Species 2:** *Ballparkius nonsensicalus*
> This species allows you to eliminate answer choices containing numbers that are obviously too high or too low.

Both species can be found on the Math test, as well as in shaded, woodland areas. Their diets consist of tubers, roots, and students who rush through multiple-choice questions. Species 1, *Numeralis eliminatorius*, is especially fond of catching students, who, when confused by a question, pick the answer choice that has identical numbers to those in the original question. If captured and trained, both POE species make excellent test-taking techniques.

Here's an example of *Numeralis eliminatorius* in its native habitat.

2. Prakash is assembling a crib for his nephew. He tries a $\frac{3}{8}$-inch screw in one of the legs, but discovers that is it slightly too large. Which of the following screw sizes is the next smaller one?

A. $\frac{1}{8}$ inch

B. $\frac{5}{16}$ inch

C. $\frac{1}{2}$ inch

D. $\frac{5}{8}$ inch

Here it would be easy to fall prey to *Numeralis eliminatorius*: You look at the question and try to solve the calculations in your head, leaving the paper blank. Nothing comes to mind, so with a quick glance at the answer choices you see A and D, both of which contain 8 in the denominator. Since 8 was in the original question ($\frac{3}{8}$-inch screw), you pick A or D and then rush off. You have just been eaten by *Numeralis*!

> Remember to go through the Math test twice. Save the hard or time-consuming questions for the second pass.

If you have no idea how to solve this question, your best bet would be to rule out choices A and D and then guess. (If you'd rather solve it mathematically, find a common denominator (16) for all the fractions; so $\frac{3}{8}$ becomes $\frac{6}{16}$, $\frac{1}{8}$ becomes $\frac{2}{16}$, $\frac{5}{16}$ stays unchanged, etc. You'll see that choice B is just slightly smaller than the $\frac{6}{16}$- (or $\frac{3}{8}$-) inch screw.

Strategy

Be wary of any answer choice that contains the same numbers as those in the question stem. They're often traps designed to trick you if you hurry.

The other species of POE, *Ballparkius nonsensicalus*, can be found in the question below.

3. A hat contains 90 slips of paper that are blue, red, or yellow. If half the slips are yellow, and the ratio of blue slips to red slips is 2 to 1, how many red slips are there?

    A. 60

    B. 45

    C. 30

    D. 15

Common sense can help uncover the incorrect *Ballparkius* answers. First, there are a few things you can ask yourself to determine the general ballpark of the answer. If half the slips are yellow, then how many yellow slips are there? The answer is half of 90, which is 45. That leaves 45 slips of either red or blue paper. With this in mind, do you think the number of red slips is greater or less than 45?

Common sense should tell you that there have to be fewer than 45 red slips of paper. That means A and B are both wrong. Choice A is way off, since it's greater than 45. By estimating the correct answer, you used POE to eliminate *Ballparkius* answer choices.

Look at the two remaining answer choices, C and D. The question states, "the ratio of blue slips to red slips is 2 to 1." So which one would you pick? If you choose D, 15, you'd be right—since 30 blue slips outnumber 15 red slips by 2 to 1.

Strategy

When working the math questions, POE is your most effective tool

The Big Five Question Types

Though it's impossible to describe *exactly* what will appear on the Math test, it is possible to predict much of content that will covered. This is because the GHSGT is a standardized test designed to see how well Georgia students are mastering the state curriculum. Many of the questions you'll see will fall into five question types—what we call the *Big Five*.

Familiarize yourself with the examples listed below, but be prepared to improvise on the actual test: Invariably there will be some variation in the question types.

The Math content strands are:

• Number and Computation

• Data Analysis

• Measurement and Geometry

• Algebra

1. Number Sense Questions

These questions test your understanding of a variety of basic math terms. Favorite topics include: percentages, number lines, mean and median, fractions, ratios, exponents, order of operations, greater than/less than, positive and negative numbers, and number lines. If you just said, "Huh?" to any of these topics, your first order of business is to review them intimately.

Strategy

Questions involving simple math terms do in fact become "simple" if you're familiar with the terms being used.

4. Listed below is the distribution of students at Cloverleaf High who are taking a foreign language.

French	44%
Spanish	34%
German	20%
Urdu	2%

If 550 students take a foreign language, how many of them are taking French?

A. 308

B. 242

C. 110

D. 17

5. $(2 + 3 \times \sqrt{25})^2$ equals

    A. 100

    B. 289

    C. 625

    D. 900

Question 4 is a fairly straightforward percentage question. If you are familiar with percentages, you know to multiply the total number of students (550) by the percentage taking French (44%, or 0.44). This gives you 242, choice B. But if you're in the mood to use POE, you can eliminate some *Ballparkius* choices. For instance, half, or 50%, of 550 is 275. Since you're looking for 44%, you know the answer needs to be slightly less than 275. Choice A is way too big, and D is too small, leaving B and C. A good guess should lead you right to B.

Question 5 tests your knowledge of the proper *order of operations*. Just plugging the numbers into the calculator from left to right will yield 625, but this is incorrect. You have to do it in the right order of operations, which is: *Parentheses* first, then *Exponents*, then *Multiplication and Division* (left to right), and last, *Addition and Subtraction* (left to right). In fact, the *25* in the question indicates that this is a bit of *Numeralis eliminatorius*. Take the square root of 25, multiply it by 3, and then add 2. Then, square that number to get choice B, 289.

Knowing your basic math terms is the key to solving Number Sense questions.

2. Chart/Graph Questions

The Math test will be filled with questions involving graphs and charts. The easiest of these merely ask you to interpret some data. Harder ones involve reading the data and then doing something with that information. The hardest questions ask you to choose the graph that best represents a particular situation.

6. The graph below shows amount of money earned by Anju and Jonas while working at a pizzeria.

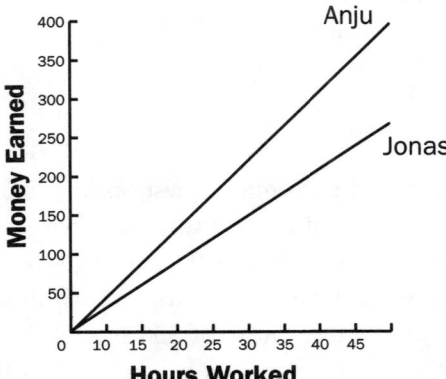

Based on the graph, which of the following is true?

A. Jonas works more hours than Anju each week.

B. Jonas makes more money per hour than Anju does.

C. Anju could work fewer hours and still earn as much money as Jonas each week.

D. Even if Jonas worked the same number of hours as Anju, he could never make the same amount of money she does.

7. If Anju and Jonas both work 20 hours one week, what is the best estimate of the mean amount of money earned by them?

A. $300

B. $200

C. $150

D. $100

8. If management decided that Anju would be paid a flat rate of $400 a week, and that Jonas would receive a raise of $1 per hour, then which statement would be true?

 A. The slope of Anju's line would be horizontal.

 B. The slope of Jonas's line would decrease.

 C. The slopes of both Jonas and Anju's lines would increase.

 D. The slope of Anju's line would be vertical.

While you probably won't see three questions based on the same graph, you might see two consecutive questions. In any event, these questions illustrate common question types. In question 6, you're being asked simply to read the graph correctly. If you do, you should narrow it down to C or D. Give C a hard look, as *could* is an important word. C is the right answer: D is wrong if both Anju and Jonas worked 0 hours each week

In question 7, reading the graph is still important, but now you must combine that with number sense terminology, *mean*. *Mean* stands for *average*, and the average of Anju and Jonas's earnings will be the point midway between their two earnings lines, straight above 20 hours. Reading across from that point gets you approximately $100, choice D.

In question 8, you have to understand the graph well enough to realize that if Anju receives a flat rate, her payment line won't change in relation to her hours worked. That means her payment line would be a horizontal line coming out of $400. Choice A is the answer.

In order to do well on chart/graph questions, you need to be comfortable interpreting data in a visual form. A good place to find graphs is in the newspaper, especially the business section. The Internet is another place to look, as many sites undoubtedly use graphs for information. If you want to move on to the bonus level, construct your own graphs. Graph the number of canned goods in your kitchen each week, or the number of times the phone rings every day. Go to the nearby mall and make a chart indicating how

Find and analyze at least ten graphs: pie graphs, bar graphs, and line graphs. Make sure you understand what the horizontal and vertical axes represent.

many people give you a dollar when you ask them politely, or the number of people who say yes when you ask them to the prom. With these last two, you'll learn not only about graphs, you'll learn about money and love as well.

3. Problem-Solving Questions

Problem-Solving questions are usually word problems that require you to use variables to determine an answer. Fortunately, these question are often easy to recognize by their inclusion of variables. Unfortunately, POE isn't very effective with these questions. First, you can't ballpark an answer with variables. Second, all of the answer choices will have numbers from the original question. Still, knowing that POE doesn't work is important, because you'll know not to use it.

Strategy

Problem-Solving questions are often recognized by the presence of variables. Before you do anything else, identify on paper what each variable represents.

9. Bernie's Discount Emporium sells three types of lawn chair. The small version is $45, the large version is $74, and the deluxe chair is $145. The store sold $645 worth of lawn chairs in January. If s is the number of small lawn chairs sold, l is the number of large lawn chairs sold, and d is the number of deluxe chairs sold, which algebraic equation below represents the amount received in January for lawn chair sales?

A. $45s + 74l - 145d = 645$

B. $74s + 45l + 145d = 645$

C. $45d + 74l = 645 + 145s$

D. $645 = 74l + 145d + 45s$

Lots of writing, lots of variables = Problem-Solving question. There are three variables in this question, and if you keep track of what each one represents, you should be able to find the right answer. Going one variable at a time, *s* stands for the small chairs worth $45, so we can cross out any answer choice that doesn't combine s with 45. That gets rid of B and C, so now it's a fifty-fifty chance between A and D. In both those choices, *s, l,* and *d* are properly aligned with their respective prices, but to describe the total $645 received on lawn chair sales, you would add the amounts received from the three types of chair. In A, the money from the deluxe lawn chairs is *subtracted*, so it's incorrect. That leaves D, your answer.

Go one step at a time, don't get flustered by the extensive writing, keep track of your variables, and Problem-Solving questions will be at your mercy.

4. Geometry Questions

Along with Chart/Graph questions, Geometry questions are among the most prevalent on the GHSGT. Of course, geometry is a broad category that covers a lot of information, but if you want to narrow your focus a bit, then look at the list below:

Favorite Geometry Categories:
- measure of angles
- perimeter and area
- questions involving circles and degrees
- triangles, triangles, triangles.

Most of the Geometry questions that will appear on the test will be accompanied by a figure. The first thing you should do after reading the question is to try to ballpark (get a rough idea of) the answer.

10. When the clock is at 4:44, what is the angle between the minute hand and the hour hand?

A. 168 degrees

B. 122 degrees

C. 90 degrees

D. 60 degrees

Look at the hands of the clock and ask yourself, "Is that angle *greater* or *less* than 90 degrees?" A right angle is 90 degrees, and since the hands here are clearly set at an angle more than 90 degrees, you can cross out C and D. They're too small. Now, take a guess, or do the math. B is the answer.

Strategy

On Geometry questions that have diagrams, try using your eyes to ballpark the answer. This can work with both angles and lengths.

For the most part, the Geometry questions that appear on the test will be a bit esoteric.

11. A triangle has two sides that are 7 cm and 9 cm. Which of the following cannot be the third side?

A. 2 cm

B. 4 cm

C. 7 cm

D. 14 cm

Questions like this are why you'll want to know everything there is to know about triangles before you take the test. For this question, use POE first: What can you eliminate? If you said C, then good for you! It's that pesky *Numeralis eliminatorius* again.

Barring a math epiphany, attack question 11 by attempting to sketch the answer choices freehand—but with the right proportions. Draw a triangle with sides of 7 cm, 9 cm, and 2 cm (choice A). Can you do it (without bending time and space)? Probably not, since you need more than 2 cm to connect 7 cm and 9 cm lines and still have a triangle. Since 2 cm cannot be the third side, A is your answer.

Strategy

Know all that you can about the favorite geometry categories, and be prepared to use that information.

5. Probability Questions

1. What are the odds that you'll encounter at least one probability on the Math test?

   A. Pretty good

   B. About 10 in 25 or 6 to 4

   C. No chance at all

   D. What are "odds"?

Hopefully, you picked A here. There's a pretty good chance you'll be faced with a probability question. There are two basic types:

   Type 1: Either you figure out all the different possible combinations, or

   Type 2: You figure out the odds of an event's occurring

In type 1, the trick is to think multiplication.

12. The following action figures are sold at a nearby store:

Soldiers	Dinosaurs	Villains	Superheroes
Capt. Bob	Stegosaurus	Dr. Footlock	Mr. Goodness
Audie	Sleestack	Goobertor	Ariadne Jones
Sgt. Mekmek	Cerotopus	Skimjeevil	
	Dimetrodon		

If you went to the store and bought one of each type of action figure, how many different combinations could be made?

A. 72

B. 36

C. 12

D. 4

The phrase *how many different combinations* indicates you're dealing with the first type of probability question. Finding an answer for this type of question always involves multiplication. The fundamental counting principle: If there are *m* ways one even can happen and *n* ways a second event can happen, then there are *m* × *n* ways for the two evens to happen.

So, for this question, list all the different types of action figure, and then multiply them together.

3 soldiers x 4 dinosaurs x 3 villains x 2 superheroes =
3   x   4   x   3   x   2   = 72, answer A

For the second type of probability question, the *what are the odds* type, you'll need to find two key numbers: the number of favorable outcomes, and the total number of possible outcomes in which a specific event will occur.

$$\text{Probability} = \frac{\text{Favorable Outcomes}}{\text{Total Number of Possible Outcomes}}$$

Now look at question 13, which is similar to an earlier question.

13. A hat contains 90 slips of paper that are either blue, red, or yellow. Half of the slips are yellow, and the ratio of blue slips to red slips is 2 to 1. If one slip is chosen at random, what is the probability that it is red?

   A. $\frac{1}{2}$

   B. $\frac{1}{3}$

   C. $\frac{1}{6}$

   D. $\frac{1}{12}$

The first number we need to find is the total number of possible outcomes, which we're given as 90, the total number of slips. The second number we'll need is the number of favorable outcomes in question, that is, the number of red slips. To do this, we want to first find how many yellow slips there are. We know that half the slips are yellow (45 slips), so that means there are 45 slips remaining. Since the ratio of blue slips to red slips is 2 to 1, this means there are 30 blue and 15 red slips. So 15 is our second number, which we must now place over our first number, 90. This gives you $\frac{15}{90}$, or reduced, $\frac{1}{6}$, choice C.

Strategy

On "how many different combinations" questions, think *multiplication*. On "what are the odds" questions, find the two numbers needed to represent the probability (total number of outcomes and number of desired outcomes.)

This concludes the math discussion. Remember, if you ever feel like you're getting in way too deep on a question, just shout "man dubáunnu!" which means "I'm drowning!" in Nepalese. A lifeguard will come by shortly to rescue you.

Chapter 5

SCIENCE

HOW THE SCIENCE TEST IS LIKE
THE KREBS CYCLE AND RIDING A BICYCLE

Imagine Person A and Person B are sitting on a couch one Saturday afternoon. They have the option of either staying where they are and watching *World's Best Bowling Mistakes* for the third time or going outside for a bike ride. Person A decides to go for a nice five-mile spin around the neighborhood, but person B opts to stay on the couch and watch that one scene where the person accidentally eats the ten pin, confusing it for an oblong sourdough sandwich.

Based on this information, who do you think will use more energy and burn more calories, person A, riding a bike, or person B, sitting on the couch? Chances are, you'll guess A, and that's right, since everyone knows that physical labor takes more energy than being a couch potato. It's just common sense. Now, here's the bonus question: What is the Krebs cycle, and how would riding a bike affect it?

That question is a little tougher to answer, so here's some help. The Krebs cycle is the name for a chemical reaction in the human body that converts food into energy. So riding a bike would cause an increase in the Krebs cycle since more energy is needed for that activity. This explanation is fine and dandy, but here's the most important point: You didn't need to know a thing about the Krebs cycle in order to know that person A used more energy than person B.

> ### Strategy
>
> On the Science test, you won't always need to know the exact scientific terms in order to grasp how something works.

To put it another way, common sense is often all you need to answer a GHSGT science question. For instance, you didn't need to know what the Krebs cycle was to know that riding a bike uses more energy than sitting on a couch. So don't think that you have to be Albert Einstein to do well on this section. Sure, being Einstein would help, but you can still get a decent score if you think of yourself as Einstein's younger brother or sister, who doesn't know all the proper scientific terms but has a lot of common sense.

Using the Krebs cycle, a man rides through town.

Science Test Facts

The Science test includes 70 questions (plus an additional 10 field-test questions), broken down into three content categories.

Content	Percentage of Test
1. Process/Research Skills	30–32%
2. Physical Science	33–35%
3. Biology	33–35%

The three content areas cover a broad range of topics: *Process/Research Skills* will test processes and skills common to all areas of science. That includes using resources, designing experiments, and interpreting data presented in tables and charts. *Physical Science* covers all areas of physical science, including chemical concepts. Topics will include properties of matter, electricity, acids and bases, force, work, wave motion, and energy transfer. *Biology* will test your knowledge of the cellular basis of life, animal and plant systems, reproduction, genetics, classification schemes, ecology, and environmental conservation.

The Big Four Question Types

As you can see from the content description above, the three content areas in science cover a much wider range of topics than do the other subject tests. But don't despair! Learn the following techniques, and you'll be better prepared for this section than most students.

1. Common Sense/POE Questions

Never underestimate the amount of scientific knowledge you actually have. Look at the following question.

1. Temperature and _____ are two primary factors that determine the brightness of a star as seen from Earth.
   A. density

   B. radioactivity

   C. distance

   D. water content

Scan the answer choices and ask yourself, "If there's a light far away, what would affect how bright it is?" Choices A and B are nice scientific terms, but how would they affect the brightness of a light? Imagine a person is holding a lantern 100 feet away from you. What would make the light brighter? If that person moved 50 feet closer, wouldn't the light be brighter? If you think the answer is yes—and you should—then you have the answer, choice C, distance.

Common sense can be applied to many science questions. It often helps to restate the problem into simpler terms. Changing a question about the brightness of a star billions of miles away into one about the brightness of a lantern being held nearby makes it easier to think about. If follows, then, that finding the correct answer will become easier as well.

2. Heat absorbed by the earth during the day is radiated into space at night. This cooling is least likely to occur on a night when it is
   A. clear and dry.

   B. windy and rainy.

   C. cloudy and calm.

   D. cloudy and windy.

Even if you're not an expert at radiational cooling, you still have at least a one-in-four chance of getting this problem right, and a little POE could help those odds even more. Ask yourself, "Which factors would help release heat?" When you're outside, does a breeze help cool you off? Of course it does, since a breeze helps circulate air and keeps the temperature from steadily rising in one place (it also causes high pressure cooler air to flow into areas with low pressure warm air). This means you can eliminate B and D.

The earth would probably be cooled off by winds in the same way you're cooled off by them. That leaves A and C, so take a guess. If you think that clouds might act like a blanket around the earth, preventing it from cooling off, you would guess choice C, which is the right answer.

Strategy

Try mixing the scientific property know as "common sense" with POE in a 1:1 ratio. It's a sure formula for success!

2. Visual Information Questions

A picture is worth a thousand words. It's also worth a lot of points on the Science test, since several questions are sure to have a visual component. This visual information might be in the form of a map, chart, graph, etcetera. Visual Information questions in science are a lot like those in math, and certain strategies can be effectively applied to both subject areas.

| Bucket 1 | Bucket 2 | Bucket 3 | Bucket 4 |

3. The four buckets above contain samples of sand, silt, and pebbles. Which bucket shows the most likely settling pattern of the contents?

    A. Bucket 1

    B. Bucket 2

    C. Bucket 3

    D. Bucket 4

One thing is for certain: You wouldn't want to drink the contents of any of the buckets. Beyond that, which of the three objects—sand, silt, or pebbles— is heaviest? It stands to reason that the heaviest particles will settle at the bottom, while the lightest will go to the top.

Since pebbles are the heaviest, they'll most likely be at the bottom of the bucket. Look at your answer choices, and eliminate any choices that don't have pebbles at the bottom. This eliminates A, B, and D. Choice C is your answer.

Strategy

When visual information accompanies a question, look at the picture to find the answer. A graph or chart is never there just to add interest; rather, it's the key to finding the answer.

While these questions will ask you about some scientific topic, the test makers are really examining how well you can decipher the visual information. This is good news, since it means a graph question about aqueous solutions is just a basic graph question. You would be able to answer it if you're good at graph questions—regardless of how knowledgeable you are about aqueous solutions. In other words, your expertise at a test-taking skill (reading graphs and deciphering visual information) can help you overcome a limitation in scientific knowledge.

3. Research/Experiment questions

Questions in this category roughly correlate with the *Process/Research Skills* content strand. Among other things, these questions test your ability to read and interpret maps, charts, models, and other scientific imagery (such as reading a barometer, microscope, scale). You will also be tested on common scientific tools, such as beakers and microscopes. Which one of these would you use to hold hydrochloric acid, and which would you use to examine bacteria? If you can't answer this question, you'll end up with an acid-etched microscope and an incorrect answer.

Another focus of the Research/Experiment questions is your ability to create and interpret scientific experiments.

4. Jonas wants to find out if the rainfall in his town is becoming acid rain. The best way for him to collect this information would be to

   A. gather one sample on one rainy day.

   B. gather one sample on several rainy days.

   C. gather several samples on one rainy day.

   D. gather several samples on several rainy days.

The more information you have, the better you can prove an experiment. If Jonas had only one rain sample, who's to say there isn't something strange about that sample? Or if he had several samples from only one day, perhaps something occurred that day to throw his readings off. But if he had numerous samples over a period of time, and they all showed the same thing, then Jonas would be able to make a more accurate prediction. On question 4, then, the best answer is D, since Jonas would have the greatest number of samples.

Strategy

Make sure you understand the basic elements of scientific experimentation before Test Day.

4. Jargon Questions

Barring questions about common sense and visual information, many problems on the test will examine your knowledge of science and scientific terms. In other words, how well do you know your science "lingo" and processes?

5. Which of the following gases is not the result of natural processes?

   A. carbon dioxide

   B. ozone

   C. adenosine triphosphate

   D. chlorofluorocarbons

Even if you don't know the precise answer here, the extent to which you know scientific terms can help you use POE. For instance, you might look at the answer choices and realize that C is not even a gas, so it won't be the answer. When you exhale (a natural process!), you breathe out carbon dioxide, a fact you might know, so that means A can't be the answer. That leaves B or D—take a guess.

Have you heard about the *ozone layer*? You might know that it's part of our natural environment. (It's an atmospheric layer that blocks most solar ultraviolet radiation from entering the lower atmosphere.) Choice C is part of the Krebs cycle, so D, chlorofluorocarbons, must be the answer.

As you can see, the more you know about scientific terms, the better your chances of doing well—so brush up as much as you can. Even though the range of science topics that appears on the test is quite broad, there are some recurring themes you would do well to review.

Science Favorites

1. **Parts of a Cell**—mitochondria, RNA, DNA, and the other parts of a basic cell

2. **Basic Genetics**—dominant and recessive genes, and how they combine

3. **Basic Knowledge about Elements, i.e. the periodic chart**—simple formulas about how elements combine, and general information about metals, gases, and liquids

4. **Parts of an Atom**—neutrons, protons, and electrons, and how these particles interact (periodic chart questions in this category might ask about atomic weight).

While these topics are broad, you'll be in good shape if you understand the Big Picture and the important terms for each. For *Parts of a Cell*, you won't need to know about cellular mutations in prokaryotic bacteria, you'll just need to know the main parts of the cell and the functions they perform.

Common sense, combined with general knowledge about the topics above, will help you get through most of the Science questions. Of course, some questions won't have any visual information for you to use, and they won't be very susceptible to POE; keep in mind that these problems will be tough for all students, not just for you. So don't get upset when you come to a really challenging question: Take your best shot and move on.

> As reference material, your Science test will include a *periodic chart.*

When Test Day is over, go out and blow off some steam by going for a bike ride. Tell your parents you're going out "to convert some acetyl groups into adenosine triphosphate and guanosine triphosphate" but that they shouldn't worry because you promise not to "lose any oxaloacetate." Then, rush out the door before they recover from shock.

SOCIAL STUDIES

HOW HISTORY ON THE GHSGT IS LIKE DRAWING A RAINBOW WITH A 16-, 64-, OR 128-PIECE BOX OF CRAYONS

When it comes to drawing a rainbow with crayons, there's a world of difference between using a 16-piece and a 128-piece set. With a 16-piece set, that shift from yellow to green is hard to pull off, and the transition from indigo to violet is nearly impossible. Sure, you can draw a rainbow, but it might not stay even two months on the family fridge.

On the other hand, a 128-piece set allows you to draw an incredibly exact rainbow, with subtle shading throughout. You'll have some colors, like Wackberry Blue and Nonchalant Pumpkin, that you won't even know what to do with. A rainbow drawn that many colors will stay on the fridge for a long time, and might even make it into the family album.

On the Social Studies GHSGT, many of the questions are straightforward and precise, testing your knowledge of historical facts. For example, "Who wrote the Declaration of Independence?" How well you do on these questions depends primarily on how much history and geography you know. In other words, do you have a 16-piece knowledge or a 128-piece knowledge of history? Clearly, the more you know, the better. If you don't know a lot of history, well, things can get tough—as tough as drawing a rainbow with only 16 colors.

This chapter will help you focus on some of the major historical facts you'll want to study for the test. By doing so, you should be able to bolster your knowledge of history enough so that you go into the test with a 64-piece box of historical knowledge. Granted, that's only half the 128-piece box, but 64 pieces is a lot more than 16 pieces. Your goal is to know enough history to earn a passing score. It doesn't have to be a great score, though that would be nice; you just want a rainbow nice enough to do well on the exam.

Social Studies Test Facts

The Social Studies test contains 80 questions (plus an additional 10 field-test questions), broken down into six content categories.

Content	Percentage of Test
1. World Studies	18–20%
2. U.S. History to 1865	18–20%
3. U.S. History since 1865	18–20%
4. Civics/Citizenship	12–14%
5. Map and Globe Skills	15%
6. Information Processing Skills	15%

The Social Studies test shares certain characteristics with the other subject tests:

1. As on the Science test, you don't always need to know the precise historical fact in order to get a problem right.

2. As on the Math and Science tests, there will be charts and graphs, and the skills you'll need to analyze them are the same for all subjects.

3. As on the English/Language Arts test, your reading passage skills will be necessary for some questions.

4. As on all subject tests, POE is still your friend.

In spite of the similarities the Social Studies test has with the other subject tests, there is one big difference: While POE can be used here, you will need to concretely know some history and geography. This is similar to the Science test, but it's even harder here. Most students know something about basic scientific phenomena like sunlight or electricity, but this isn't always the case with social studies and history. If you don't know who the president was during World War II, no amount of everyday experience will be able to help you figure it out. So at a minimum, you need to know the basics. Once you have them down, you'll be in a position to use POE effectively. For instance:

1. In the sixteenth century, one effect of European contact with the Americas was
   A. a rich flowering of trade between Spain and the ancient Maya civilization.
   B. widespread slaughter of North American buffalo by European settlers.
   C. a surge in Native American populations.
   D. a huge influx of wealth into Europe from the New World.

Whether or not you can use POE here is a function of what you know about the European impact on the New World. The diseases carried by Christopher Columbus and others wiped out millions of Native Americans, so C is wildly wrong. Choice B, widespread slaughter of buffalo, was done (by Americans) much later than the sixteenth century, so that's out. We're left with A and D. Either take a guess or remember that the Spanish and others took tons of gold from the New World, primarily through plunder. The answer is D.

The Big Three Question Types

1. Map Questions: Here There'll Be Dragons

Since 15 percent of the test is devoted to map and globe skills, rest assured that you'll see some maps! Consider the following question.

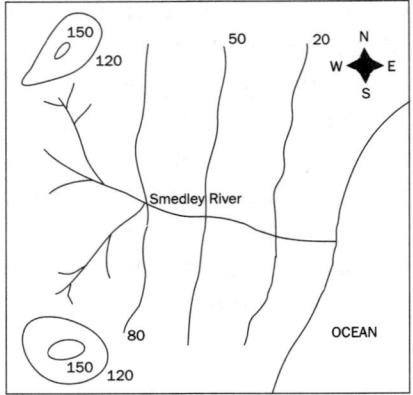

2. According to the topographic map above, the Smedley River flows in what direction?

A. North

B. South

C. East

D. West

You don't need to be a riverologist—or whatever you call someone who knows about rivers—in order to get this problem right. You just need to use some common sense when looking at the map. For instance, the Smedley River crosses the map in a fairly straight line, so we can eliminate choices A and B. Using your eyes, you can see the river isn't going in either of those directions.

At this point, you could either guess or look at the elevation numbers on the map. The higher numbers are on the left side of the map, and since water flows downhill, C must be the answer.

Of course, knowing about topographic maps beforehand would have helped you immensely on this question.

Strategy

Go to a library, find the most comprehensive atlas, and look at the kinds of maps it has.

Look for and examine political maps, cultural maps, economic maps, and even weather maps. Make sure you learn to recognize the symbols used to denote rivers, mountains, salt marshes, glaciers, and other physical features. If you become comfortable reading these things before Test Day, these Map and Globe questions should fall into your map—I mean, *lap*.

3. Which number on the map corresponds to the location of the Aztec Empire in 1400?

   A. 1

   B. 2

   C. 3

   D. 4

This is a part geography, part world history question. If you know about this ancient civilization, you'll be able to go straight to choice A.

2. Key Topic Questions

On the previous Aztec question, you didn't need to know about Aztec farming techniques, or whether the Aztecs used a primitive form of the Dewey Decimal system. What you needed were the basic facts about that society. If you knew where the Aztec people lived, the answer was easy. This is primarily what Key Topic questions require: Construct a 64-piece crayon set, and get the Big Picture.

The test makers don't expect you to know everything there is to know about history and social studies. What they do expect you to have is the Big Picture for the major topic areas.

What follows are some key topics that will likely appear on this test. Be sure to acquaint yourself with each topic well ahead of time, reviewing the main facts and pertinent issues. You don't need to spend four hours each night on them, nor should you pull a historical fact all-nighter. Instead, plan your time well, so that you can absorb the information in a reasonable amount of time. Combined with the other test-taking strategies (common sense, POE, two-pass approach), the knowledge you have about these topics should enable you to answer many Social Studies questions.

Key Topic A: The War Checklist

It's quite likely that you'll see questions on the following wars: the American Revolution, the Civil War, World Wars I and II. Since wars are such catastrophic events, they inevitably leave large historical footprints. To help you focus in on the Big Picture of each war, use the following checklist.

1. Who fought on which sides? What were the opposing sides called?

2. During what years did the war occur?

3. What were the causes of the war?

4. Who were the political leaders of the countries involved?

5. When and how did the war end?

6. What were the major battles/events?

7. What were some of the social side effects of the war?

8. Who won?

If you can answer all of these questions, you'll be armed with the basics needed to tackle most war-related questions. At the very least, this should provide you with enough information to optimally use POE.

Key Topic B: World Studies

Many World Studies questions include a geographical component, as did the Aztec Empire question. For those questions that are specifically historical, look over the following subjects:

- the Renaissance and the Reformation
- European colonization
- the Industrial Revolution
- Communism and the Cold War

Key Topic C: U.S. History to 1865

This area includes the American Revolution and the Civil War

- the American Colonies
- Declaration of Independence
- George Washington
- Creation of a nation (such as the Louisiana Purchase)

Key Topic D: U.S. History from 1865

This area includes World Wars I and II:

- expansion into the West (railroads)
- segregation and the Jim Crow Laws
- the Great Depression
- the Civil Rights Movement

Key Topic E: Civics/Citizenship

There will be only a few civics and citizenship questions on the test. You need to understand the basic functions of government (local, state, and national), the role of the citizen, and individual rights and responsibilities.

3. Reading Passage Questions

Reading Passage Questions appear in the *Information Processing Skills* strand. You will be presented with a prompt or stimulus that provides information in the form of a graphic or chart. You will then read a 50–200 word passage and then answer related questions. You may be asked to identify the main idea of a passage, to separate fact from fiction, or to interpret a chart. Because these questions will require some time to work through, you might want to save them for your second pass through the test. Once you actually jump in to solve them, these questions should be fairly straightforward. Make sure to look in the passage for the answers.

Strategy

On Reading Passage Questions, be sure to glance at the questions first, before you begin reading the passage. That way, as you read, you can look for the answer.

Use your knowledge of history along with the information that's given to attack the following question.

Speaker 1: People in Western Europe were persecuting my family and me because of our religion, so we took a boat and came to the New World. We eventually settled in the St. Lawrence River area.

Speaker 2: In search of glory along the frontier, I saw in ad in the paper that talked about a colony that Stephen Austin was starting on Mexican territory. I left Virginia to move there.

Speaker 3: When gold was discovered at Sutter's Mill, I left my home in the Appalachian Mountains and went to find my fortune.

Speaker 4: A glass merchant by trade, I left Germany for the New World. Since my glassware was fairly expensive, I decided to set up shop in one of the larger metropolitan centers along the east coast.

4. Speaker 2 settled in which location?
   A. California

   B. New York

   C. Quebec

   D. Texas

This question illustrates why reading a question before delving into the passage is a good idea. As you can see, you have to read only the text for speaker 2, since that's all the question asks about. The rest of the speakers are included merely to provide incorrect answer choices, and to take up your time.

So, what's the correct answer? Well, you might know that "Mexican territory" included neither New York nor Quebec, so B and C are out. That leaves A and D, and since Austin is the capital of Texas, D is your best bet.

Learning key historical facts, combined with your knowledge of charts and reading passage skills, should be enough to get you a decent score on this exam. You should be able to approach each question and have a good chance of solving it. Just remember that the right answer will always be there, waiting for you like a pot of gold at the end of a nicely drawn rainbow.

Chapter 7

RESULTS

UNDERSTANDING LIFE AND YOUR GHSGT SCORES (LIFE NOT INCLUDED)

At last, a chapter title that speaks for itself!

Your score is based on the number of questions that you get right. Any wrong questions, or questions left blank, are not deducted.

The score range for each subject test is 400–600 points. A minimum passing score on all tests, is 500 points. The score breakdown for each subject is as follows:

Subject Test	Fail	Pass	Pass Plus*
English	400–499	500–537	538–600
Math	400–499	500–534	535–600
Science	400–499	500–530	531–600
Social Studies	400–499	500–525	526–600

* *Pass Plus* indicates mastery of the subject.

> For the latest test information, check out the Georgia Department of Education's Website at:
> **www.doe.k12.ga.us/sla/ret/ghsgt.asp**.

For the Writing test, the two graders will assign a score of 1–4 to each of the four domains (*Content/ Organization, Style, Conventions of Written Language, and Sentence Formation*). *Content/Organiza-tion* is worth twice as much as the other domains. As is the case with the other subject tests, the minimum passing score for the Writing test is 500.

Your raw scores will be mathematically converted to scaled scores. Scaled scores take into account the fact that some questions are harder than others, giving more weight to some questions and less weight to others. Your score report will include an overall scaled score as well as subscores of your performance in each content area.

While a low score can be cause for concern, it isn't necessarily an indication that you're lagging far behind in your studies. Keep these scores in perspective. If you don't pass every subject test the first time around, remember that you're not alone! Many Georgia students fail one or two subject tests on their first administration.

Note: If you do not pass all the required tests but have met all other gradua-tion requirements, you may be eligible for a *Certificate of Performance* or a *Special Education Certificate*. With one of these certificates, you'll be able to leave high school with your class. However, in order to qualify for a high school diploma, you must return within two years to retake the relevant subject tests.

> While earning a *Pass Plus* designation is nice, your main goal is to pass the test. Don't be overly concerned about getting every question right.

In terms of how the GHSGT is scored, this is the end of the story. But end of story in this instance only means *end of discussion on how you scored on one stan-dardized test*. This test should be seen for what it is—an interesting checkpoint along a very long highway. Some students who score at the lowest level on this test will go on to graduate from prestigious universities with advanced degrees, while others who score at the highest level will struggle to finish high school. Your scores simply highlight the areas in which you need improvement. So regardless of how you do, try not to lose confidence in yourself or doubt your ability to succeed. Of all the advice given in this book, nothing is more important—or more accurate—than that.

How Did We Do? Grade Us.

Thank you for choosing a Kaplan book. Your comments and suggestions are very useful to us. Please answer the following questions to assist us in our continued development of high-quality resources to meet your needs.

The Kaplan book I read was: _____

My name is: _____

My address is: _____

_____

My e-mail address is: _____

What overall grade would you give this book?   Ⓐ Ⓑ Ⓒ Ⓓ Ⓕ

How relevant was the information to your goals?   Ⓐ Ⓑ Ⓒ Ⓓ Ⓕ

How comprehensive was the information in this book?   Ⓐ Ⓑ Ⓒ Ⓓ Ⓕ

How accurate was the information in this book?   Ⓐ Ⓑ Ⓒ Ⓓ Ⓕ

How easy was the book to use?   Ⓐ Ⓑ Ⓒ Ⓓ Ⓕ

How appealing was the book's design?   Ⓐ Ⓑ Ⓒ Ⓓ Ⓕ

What were the book's strong points? _____

How could this book be improved? _____

Is there anything that we left out that you wanted to know more about?

Would you recommend this book to others?   ☐ YES   ☐ NO

Other comments: _____

_____

_____

Do we have permission to quote you?   ☐ YES   ☐ NO

Thank you for your help. Please tear out this page and mail it to:

Dave Chipps, Managing Editor
Kaplan Educational Centers
888 Seventh Avenue
New York, NY 10106

Or, you can answer these questions online at www.kaplan.com/talkback.

Thanks!